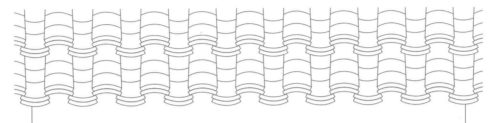

HISTORIC HOUSES IN FUJIAN

//////////////////////////

• ANCIENT VILLAGES

Qu Liming / Chen Wenbo

福建经典古民居

古村

上

摄影 \ 曲利明

撰文 \ 陈文波

海峡出版发行集团

海峡书局

远去的田园牧歌（代前言）

1 村落是什么? 是我们的根。

无论我们现在人在何处，身在何方，追根溯源，我们或者我们的先辈都来自村落。

人是一种群居动物，而村落是人类聚落发展中的一种低级形式，当然，也是走向高级聚落——城市的必经形式。我们国家是个农耕大国，我们走出来的村落，也被称为农村。直到今天，这些农村依然承载了我们乃至我们家族的记忆、历史和传承，也是今天生活在城市中大多数人的乡愁所在。

村落中，最有价值的无疑是传统村落。

我搜索了一下，对于传统村落，网络上是这么定义的：又称古村落，指村落形成较早，拥有较丰富的文化与自然资源，具有一定历史、文化、科学、艺术、经济、社会价值，应予以保护的村落。传统村落中蕴藏着丰富的历史信息和文化景观，是中国农耕文明留下的最大遗产。

既然被称为遗产，我们能继承的，还有几分？

依稀记得，我们的乡村，在文人的笔下，是充满了田园牧歌般的诗意：远山连绵，小桥流水，粉墙黛瓦，袅袅炊烟，牧童归牛……

然而，事实上，在日益加速的城市化浪潮中，这样的场景已经相当少见。我们的古村落正在以飞快的速度消失，有数据显示：从21世纪初开始，中国的城镇化发展伴随着古村落的迅速消失，从2002年到2012年的十年间，中国的自然村数量从362万个减少到273万个，十年间减少了近90万个。

同时另外一个数据表明，当前中国城镇人口的数量已经超过了农村人口，田园牧歌的时代正在远去。

基于此，我们踏上了行程。

2 我们准备绕着福建走一圈。

福建，又称八闽，地处东南一隅。自古以来，这里就是山高水远，交通极为不便。中原兵燹，衣冠南渡，几次的大迁徙中，中原文化与本地文化交织碰撞，形成了闽南文化、客家文化、畲族文化、朱子文化、红色文化等极有特色的闽文化。而历经兴衰嬗变，保留了大量形态多样、人文荟萃的传统村落。这些传统村落，就是一部民间历史的载体，保存着大量的文化元素。

有资料显示，截至2016年，福建的中国传统村落数量达到230个，加上名镇名村的数量，在全国也是位居前列，这些传统村落，跨越时间长，初步形成了福建历史文化资源体系。

在行走过程中，我们经过了一个又一个的福建传统村落，宛如穿越时空，回到一个又一个历史片段中。山水古建，人文风情不一，而带给我们冲击力的，无疑是那些遗留到今天，能量巨大的文化碎片。

说是碎片，因为，我们不得不承认，传统村落正在远去。

风水。风水二字，有人将其阐述得玄而又玄，其实，说穿了，就是居住的科学。正如住在潮湿地方的人往往会建吊脚楼，靠海的村落常常用石头造房子一个道理，人，选择自己居住的环境，是经过口耳相传的经验传承的。今天，我们走进一些历史悠久的古村落，往往会发现，村子的选址相当完美，环山抱水，相当适合居住，一些村子尽管地处深山还因地制宜地布置成了防御模样，一些村子溪中人鱼和谐相传，这是风水，也是古人的智慧。

宗祠。与现代人不同，家族，对古人而言是非常重要的存在，尤其是在宗族观念很重的福建。崇文敬祖、耕读传家常常是一个家族的最美好的愿望。在传统村落中，宗祠是最有向心力的地方，这里栖息着祖先的灵魂，也寄托着乡民的梦想。一个村落的辉煌过往，一个家族的谆谆期待，都铭刻在宗祠的牌匾上、石旗杆上。

宅院。建筑是凝固的音乐，也是凝固的历史。明代以来，由于"皇权不下乡"，中国的乡村就是一个乡绅之治的社会。致仕官员、科举落第的读书人还有中小地主构成了古代村落的乡绅阶层。国人历来崇尚"富贵不还乡，若锦衣夜行"，于是各种深宅大院就冒了出来。再加上福建这地方，天高皇帝远，各种超规格建筑层出不穷，比如有超百间房的土楼土堡，超规格使用颜色的红砖厝，留存到了今天就成了遗产。

官庙。中国人的信仰秉承着实用主义的原则，到了福建，更是"闽中多淫祀"，崇尚"生而为英，死而为灵"，只要够实用，都能建庙奉祀。于是在福建的传统村落里，可以见到大大小小不一的官庙，信仰也随着水系的延长而撒播，如闽江流域的大圣信仰、闽东地区的临水夫人信仰以及闽南地区的关帝信仰等等，而在客家地区，更有石头信仰、树信仰等等，这些民间信仰都隐藏在传统村落中，偶然一场热闹的走古事，它们统统浮出水面。

路桥。古人行善，莫过于修桥铺路。在路难行的福建，此举意义更为重大，村落中的重大事情，也莫过于此。于是，我们可以从铺路的石块上，修桥的木材上读到曾经村中人做的大事。在不少村落，一些修桥的倡议者，还被供奉进了桥中的神龛里。

风俗。一方水土一方人，不同的文化背景，不同的信仰，让不同的村落拥有别样的风俗。泰宁大源村的傩舞，连城罗坊的走古事等等，展现出来，就成了今天各自的非物质文化遗产。

此外，村落中的亭台、古树，甚至村落中出产的风物土产等，都是烙在传统村落血脉上难以磨灭的印记，遇见了，是缘分，留住了，是幸运。

我们的行程从福州出发，一路往西，接着南下，继而转北，几十个村庄走过。一方面惊艳于八闽大地拥有如此多姿多彩的传统村落，另外一方面感慨：尽管新农村建设轰轰烈烈，但人还是越来越少，村落的建筑正在变得越来越像，传统村落在"空心化"中失去个性。

在我们的镜头下，留在村子里的人越来越少，也越来越老。人是村落的灵魂，没有了灵魂，那些传统村落就是一副行将就木、垂垂老矣的空壳，哪怕外表粉饰得再富丽堂皇。

在闽西连城，还没过元宵，一些村落里的人已经匆匆忙忙，准备回城的行李，一些传统的民俗活动陷入缺乏人手的境地。

在闽北，闽江的许多源头村，仅仅只剩下几户人家。村落里没有了学校，没有了商店，在城镇化的裹挟中，农民匆匆变成城镇居民，丢下的，不仅仅是一亩三分地。

在沿海条件好一点的地区，随着钢筋水泥的侵蚀，整片的古民居里冒出一栋一栋的火柴盒一样的房子。是的，生活习惯不同了，谁也不愿意住在阴冷潮湿的旧房子里。

当然，也有被旅游拯救的村落，熙熙攘攘的客流，带来村落新的发展模式，也带来了商业化的弊端，建一架大水车，编几个故事，效果立竿见影，只是这强心针能持续多久，我们不好说。

青山遮不住，毕竟东流去。毫无疑问，城市化是社会发展的浪潮，但我们也需要留住我们的乡愁。我们必须承认，田园牧歌的时代已经远去。那么，能留住的只有现在。

这个现在，就是当下。

我们用影像记录现在，福建的传统村落最原始的生态，最鲜活的人文，虽然很多已经变成曾经。但我们仍然认为，这是一件很有意义的事情，毕竟，我们的曾经，是那么美丽。

所幸今天，从国家到地方，对传统村落的重视正在日益增加，中国传统村落的名录已经公布了四批；历史文化名村名镇的命名告别终身制，退出制度的建立将更大限度地保护原有的历史风貌；对于传统村落和古建筑的修缮经费正在下拨……

我们也期待，福建的传统村落一直这么美丽下去。

The Remote Arcadian Life
(an article used as the preface)

1 What is a village? It is the root of human beings. No matter where we are now, our ancestors or oursevles could trace the original hometown in the villages.

Human beings are social animals and the village is a lowgrade form of human settlement in the very beginning. And It is sure to be the only stage which must be passed by to the highgrade form of human settlement – the city. China had been a great agricultural country, therefore the settlement where we were born or grown up is called the village. Until now, the villages still preserve the memory, history and heritages of ourselves or even the families. The villages now have been the place hidden in the depth of our hearts, preserving the softest and warmest motions.

Among various villages in China, the most valuable ones should be those traditional villages. I search for the definition of the traditional village online. According to the internet, the traditional villages, also called the ancient villages, refer to the villages of a profound history, abundant cultural and natural resources that should be protected because of its various values. Those historic and cultural relics of the traditional villages actually are the biggest values of Chinese cultivation culture. What can we inherit from the villages? What 's left behind in the villages?

In the depth of the memory, the villages should be the place with meadering mountains, ancient bridges, clear running streams, white walls, grey tiles, the raising smoke from the kitchen chimney and the cowboys with returning cows...... All those in your imagination should be arcadian. But the truth is not so wonderful because of the rapid urbanizations. The pictures in the imaginations are so rare in the villages. At present, the ancient villages are in danger. According to certain statistics, at the 21st century, the unbanizations destroy a number of ancient villages. From 2002 to 2012, the natural villages had beed declined from 3.62 millions to 2.73 millions. In a decade, nearly 900,000 villages had been gone forever. At the same time, another statistics shows that the populations of the cities have already surpassed those of the villages. The arcadian times is getting further from us. Therefore, we are on the way to explore those villages scattering in the corners of Fujian Province in order to take some records of them.

2 We are going to travel around Fujian Province. Fujian Province, also called Bamin in Chinese, is located at the southeast of China. In the past, it is far away from the middle land because of incovenient transportations. Wars exploded in the middle land therefore some people escaped to Fujian for their lives. With the migrations in the history, the cultures of the middle land merge with the local ones, giving brith to various new local cultures such as Minnan Culture, Hakka Culture, She Nationality Culture, Zhuzi Culture and Red Culture. As time goes by, a great number of traditional villages with different features and rich cultures are left in Fujian Province. These traditional villages are the platforms that exhibite the history and wonderful culture.

According to certain records, there are 230 Chinese Traditional Villages in Fujian Province. The number is quite eye-catching in the nation. These villages have formed a unique historic cultural resouces system of Fujian Province.

In our route, we walked past those traditional villages one by one. When we are lost in the villages, we are taken back in the old times, savoring the history and wonderful culture. The grand architectural complexes, the landscape and the folk customs never cease to amaze us. But the most powerful things should be the cultural fragments left in the villages. The word "fragment" is applied because of the undeniable fact of the disappearance of traditional villages.

Geomancy (Fengshui in Chinese) , which is always attached to mysterious power in the nature, actually refers to the science of habitations. For example, one would choose to live in a stilted building at a moist place and the other would choose to live in a stone house by the coastal region. The way that people live is usually decided by their experiences. When we are roaming in some traditional villages, we would gasp at some perfect site selections, the complete defense system and the harmonious environment between the fish and human beings. This is the truth of geomancy which is the wisdom passed down by our ancestors.

The ancestral halls are quite common in these villages. Our ancestors, different from present people, attached great importance to the family. Advocation of cultures and honoring the ancestors have always been the most important things in the family. In the traditional villages, the ancestral halls are the most powerful places since they are the places where the ancestors rest their souls, where the villagers pray for a better life, where the glories of the villages are recorded and where the anticipations of the families are engraved. One could take a glance of the past of the families on the tablets as well as the stone poles.

The residences in the traditioanl villages have been the heritages of the history. From the Ming Dynasty to the Qing Dynasty, the villages had been ruled by country gentlemen. The retired officers, the scholars failed the imperial exams and landlords had been the members of those country gentlemen. Chinese people always prefer to show off when they are rich or famous. Therefore, these rich men and famous scholars constructed a number of great mansions in order to display their wealth and fames. Since Fujian Province is far away from the control of the imperial power, various mansions that exceeded the constructing standards of the imperial power had been built, such as the grand earthen buildings with more than hundreds of rooms and the red-brick houses. All these have been valuable heritage of human beings.

The temples, offering honors to different kinds of gods or goddesses, are the reflections of pragmatism in China. Fujianeses honor a great number of gods or goddesses since they believe these would bring them with good luck, forture and safety. In Fujian, people would build temples for brave heroes because they firmly believe that these heroes would become gods after their death. You could find a great number of temples built for gods and heroes. The believes spread along the river, such as the Monkey King belief in Minjiang River Basin, Chen Jinggu belief in Eastern Fujian District, Guan Yu belief in Southern Fujian District as well as the belief of stones or trees of Hakka people. These different gods, goddesses and heroes would gather around in the parade at certain time annually, which bring a visual feast for the people.

Roads and bridges are quite important in Fujian because of its inconvenient transportations. In the past, paving the road or setting a bridge had been the biggest kind deed of the rich or the famous. The most significant event of the villages also should be those two things. Nowadays, we could read the history on the stones and woods that made of the roads and bridges. Some people who donated money or ideas of building the bridges are even honored in the shrines.

Folk customs brings difference to the villages. Different cultural backgroud and folk believes bring villages with vigors and unique flavours. Luowu Dance in Taining Dayuan Village, Zougushi Fair in Liancheng Luofang and other folk customs now have been the well-known intangible cultural heritages.

The pavillions, ancient trees and specialties of the traditional villages are all marks of the times. If you spot them accidentaly, just cherish the beauty and indulge yourself at the very moment.

We set off in Fuzhou, heading the west first, then to the south and turning to the north at last. We have walked through thousands of villages. While we are surprised by the wonderful tradtional villages, we are also sorry to witness the declining of the traditional villages with duplicate new houses and few villages. We have to admit the truth that our villages are losing its characteristics at the process of urbanizations. In our cameras, we only have photos of the old. The truth is that the youngsters choose to leave for a better life. Without people, these villages are just a cluster of houses without the customs and culture even those houses are renovated.

We witnessed some awkward moments in the villages. Some people are rushing back to the cities before the Latern Festival when the annual folk activities should be held. In the north of Fujian, only few families choose to stay in the villages without schools and shops. With the rapid development of urbanization, the villagers are transformed to be the citizens. The things that they have left behind are not only the farmlands but also the traditional life style in the villages.

At some places, some ugly buildings stand among the ancient architectural complexes. We know that people prefer convenient life with morden facilities in new houses. And we also realize that the villages have been destroyed bits by bits. Of course, we could not deny the facts that there are certain villages which are saved by the tourism industry. Tourism brings wealth for the villages but also the disadvantages of commercialized running. Setting up a big water wheel and making up some love stories surely attract lots of tourists. But it is hard to last for long.

The wheel of times could not be stopped. Undoubtedly, urbanization is a must of the development. But for human beings, we need some place to remind ourselves of the past. We feel sorry to admit the truth that the arcadiant life are disappearing gradually. The only thing we could do is to take the record of present situations. And it is time to use the cameras to seize the precious environment as well as those vigorous folk customs. Though some of them could only be found in the pictures, we still feel it is meaningful since we preserve them in our pictures.

Luckily, our nation has realized the importance on the protections of traditonal villages and various measures have been applied to protect the original looks of the villages. We are looking forward that our traditional villages could be preserved in fine conditons in the future.

目录/CONTENTS

林浦村老街上的进士牌坊，记录古村科举时代的辉煌 / the memorial arch in the street

仓山区城门镇林浦村

　　林浦村位于福州市仓山区城门镇，又称濂浦、濂江乡，北临闽江，面向鼓山，整个村落为闽江及其支流濂江所环抱。

　　林浦村历史悠久，南宋末年，宋端宗曾驻跸于林浦村，村中的泰山宫即为宋帝行宫。林浦村历来注重文化教育，宋代朱熹讲学处"濂江书院"能保存至今，就是一个物证。在科举史上，林浦村曾出过"三代五尚书，七科八进士"的佳话，可见当地文风之鼎盛。

　　今天的林浦村，已被评为"历史文化名村"，林浦村及周边保存着大量的文物古迹，如宋代的林桥、书院，明代的牌坊、尚书家庙、尚书墓，清代的进士第、老宅等等。

Linpu Village, Chengmen Town, Cangshan District

　　Linpu Village, also called Lianpu or Lianjiangxiang, is situated in Chengmen Town, Cangshan District. Facing Gushan Mountain, this village is embraced by Minjiang River and Lianjiang River. At the end of Southern Song Dynasty, the emperor Song Duanzong once stopped by at Taishan Palace of Linpu Village to take a break. People in Linpu Village always attach great attentions to culture and education, therefore, Lianjiang College where Zhu Xi gave lectures is well-preserved. In Linpu Village, a number of high-ranking officials and candidates in the civil service examinations were emerged, which also indicated Linpu people's focus on education. Boasting abundant cultural relics such as Linqiao Bridge and the college in the Song Dynasty, memorial arches and ancestral temples of high-ranking officials in the Ming Dynasty as well as those ancient houses of candidates in the civil service examinations in the Qing Dynasty, Linpu Village is honored as the Historical and Cultural Village now.

泰山宫前有两处辕门，彰显昔日气派 / doors in front of Taishan Palace

毛主席语录，还有老式的理发店，时光的痕迹都留在这条老街上 / marks of the times

濂江书院，始建于唐末，朱熹曾在此讲学 / Lianjiang College

林尚书家庙 / the ancestral temple

林尚书家庙，记载林氏家族"三代五尚书，七科八进士"的辉煌 / the ancestral temple of a high-ranking official in the feudal time

林浦泰山宫，南宋末年曾为宋帝行宫，宋端宗曾驻跸于此 / Taishan Palace

泰山宫坐北朝南，由正殿、总管殿和天后宫三部分组成，宫内戏台、藻井，华丽异常 / Taishan Palace being comprised of the main hall, Zongguan hall and the Heavenly Goddess Palace

天后宫也是泰山宫的组成部分之一 / the Heavenly Goddess Palace

妈祖信仰在古村盛行，香火旺盛 / people in the village believing in the Heavenly Goddess

青观顶村全景，这是一个典型的平潭渔村 / the overall view of Qingguanding Village

青观顶村石头厝位于大片农田中 / stone houses among the farmland

平潭县敖东镇青观顶村

青观顶村位于平潭县敖东镇，为中国传统村落。

青观顶村是一个典型的平潭县传统渔村，村子形成于清代，三面环海，石群林立，村庄依山就势，布局灵活，在大片的农田中，石头厝错落有致，和谐美观。青观顶村的石头厝建筑保存状况较好，建筑风貌基本统一。这里石头厝从地基到墙面，从门框到梁柱基本采用周边山体的花岗岩石料，建筑外形朴素大方。

村内自然环境良好，村里的居民都很高寿，有很多老人的年龄都在90岁以上，是远近闻名的长寿村。

Qingguanding Village, Aodong Town, Pingtan County

Qingguanding Village, located in Aodong Town, is a Chinese Traditional Village. It is a traditional fishing village in Pingtan Island. The village was first established in the Qing Dynasty. The village, being surrounded by the sea, is built along the mountains. In the vast area of farmland, stone houses scatter with a picturesque disorder, making a harmonious scene. The stone houses in the village are built with nearly the same style and are preserved well. The materials of these stone houses are drawn from the mountains around the village. The natural environment are quite good therefore villagers are longevous. Most of the old are over 90 years old and it has been a famous longevity village.

青观顶村全景 / Qingguanding Village

青观顶村石头厝全部取材于本地花岗岩 / the materials of the stone house being drawn from the mountains nearby

石厝烟囱 / the chimney of the stone house

青观顶村石头厝 / the stone house in the village

青观顶村为平潭的长寿村 / the longevity village

与中国大多数村庄一样，青观顶村也面临着"空心化"问题 / the empty village

位于海边的石头厝采光较差 / the dark stone houses by the sea

尖顶教堂 / the churth with spires

白沙村全景 / Baisha Village

平潭县白青乡白沙村

　　白沙村位于平潭县白青乡，为中国传统村落。

　　白沙村地处海滨之旁，村中一排排的石头厝是最美的风景。村中有三座尖顶教堂，其中最早的白沙教堂，已有100多年的历史，教堂窗户高而尖，非常显眼。白沙村的地势较为独特，由西至东如同小山丘般逐渐降低。村落被5座山丘包围，百年来，村民们依山而建房，居然占用了近一半的山丘。村子的西边还有一片海域，称为白沙澳，海景、石头厝，再加上尖顶教堂，让白沙村多了一分异域色彩。

Baisha Village, Baiqing Country, Pingtan County

　　Baisha Village, located in Baiqing Country, Pingtan County, is a Chinese Traditioanl Village. The stone houses in the village make a wonderful view at the costal region. There are three churches with spires. Baish Church is the first to be built and has a history of more than 100 years. The windows of those churches are high and pierecing. The terrain of Baisha Village lowers from west to east as mountains. Being surrounded by 5 mountains, the village rests in the corner quietly. Villagers build their houses along the slope. To the west of the village lies the sea named Baisha'ao. The sea, the stone houses and the churches add an exotic atmosphere to the village.

白沙村石头厝屋顶 / the roof of the stone house

白沙村的石头厝紧密相连 / the stone houses being built near each other

白沙村石头厝 / the stone houses in the village

白沙村石头厝 / the stone houses in the village

石头厝内的标语，时代的印记 / the slogans in the stone houses being the mark of the times

石头厝人家 / the family in the stone house

东美村全景 / the overall view of Dongmei Village

平潭县流水镇东美村

东美村位于平潭县流水镇，为中国传统村落。

东美村，又名东尾村，在风景区东海仙境旁，这里在明代就是著名的渔港。东美村沿山而建，这里的石头厝相当有特色，墙体是古早的乱石砌法。东美村因渔而兴港，也因港而兴商，成为平潭县旧时重要的渔港、商港、军港。抗战时期，东美村是平潭的抗日据点，上演了一段传奇历史。

Dongmei Village, Liushui Town, Pingtan County

　　Dongmei Village, located in Liushui Town, is a Chinese Traditional Village. Dongmei Village, also called Dongwei Village, is near a scenic spot. In the Ming Dynasty, the village was a famous fishery harbor. The village is built along the mountain. The stone houses in the village are quite special since the walls are piled up with ripraps. The prosperity of fishery made it to be a fishery harbor while the development of the fishery harbor made it to be an important market. Therefore, this village once was quite important in the history. During the Anti-Japanese War, the village was a military base in Pingtan and played an important role at that time.

东美村形态各异的石头厝 / the diverse stone houses in the village

石头厝封火墙 / the fire seals of the stone houses

人去居空,时间无言 / the empty stone houses in the peace

古厝、古井 / the old house and the old well

老屋、老人 / the old house and the old

东美村大王宫 / Dawang Palace of Dongmei Village

东美村大王宫 / Dawang Palace in Dongmei Village

修葺一新的"大王宫" / the renovated Dawang Palace

山门村全景 / the overall view of Shanmen Village

平潭县流水镇山门村

　　山门村位于平潭县流水镇，为中国传统村落。

　　山门村，当地人俗称山门前，这个村子有700多年的历史，村中既有层层叠叠的石头古厝，还有著名的非物质文化遗产藤牌操。

　　山门村的石头厝均取材于当地，这是一种叫火成岩的石头，石质非常坚硬，不易开采。它的色彩是青墨中带黑，与我们常见的灰白色花岗岩不同。这种火成岩经过风吹日晒，慢慢地由青墨色变成了墨色，远远望去，一座座石头厝如同水墨画一样！山门村的藤牌操发源较早，迄今约有600年历史。《平潭县志》记载山门村人曾特聘水师守营教头为师，武功、舞技渐渐精进娴熟。

Shanmen Village, Liushui Town, Pingtan County

　　Shanmen Village, located in Liushui Town, is a Chinese Traditional Village. Shanmen Village, also called Shanmenqian, has a history of more than 700 years. In the village, there are stone houses as well as Tengpai Exercises which is a famous intangible cultural heritage. The stone houses are built with the petrosilexes drawn from the mountains nearby. This kind of rocks are tough and hard to explore. The color, different from common granites, is cyanine with black. Being exposed to the weather, the rock would changed its color to black. Therefore, you would find those stone houses look like those in Chinese paintings. Tengpai Exercises, with a history of about 600 years, was developed quite early. According to the records, this excercises derive from daily excercises of villagers which were taught by someone serving in the army .

山门村的石头厝有别具一格的味道 / the special flavor of the stone houses

厝顶风景 / views at the top of the houses

建在石头上的石头厝 / the stone houses built on the rocks

山门村依山而建，建筑材料全部取自当地 / the village built along the mountains with the raw material of the local

石厝风景 / the stone house

山门村的石头厝中有闽南红砖厝的风格 / the stone house of Minnan red-brick house flavour

闲坐聊家常 / chatting with villagers

山门村依然保持着传统的生活方式 / people in the village preserving a traditional life style

斗魁村石厝色彩丰富 / the colorful stone house

斗魁村全景 / the overall view of Doukui Village

平潭县苏澳镇斗魁村

　　斗魁村位于平潭县苏澳镇最北端，为中国传统村落。

　　斗魁村被七座山峦围绕，当地人把这七座山称为——金山、银山、燕山、对面山、出芦山、葫芦山、大石斗山。这七座山如同"北斗七星阵"排列，因此"斗魁村"村名也起源于此。斗魁村的石头厝也是相当有特色，与别处不同，这里的石头厝色彩斑斓，且房屋建筑略带有闽南红砖特色。站在斗魁村高处，青山碧海，海湾渔村，美不胜收。

Doukui Village, Su'ao Town, Pingtan County

　　Doukui Village, located in the north of Su'ao Town, Pingtan County, is a Chinese Traditional Village. The village is embraced by seven mountains – Jinshan Mountain, Yinshan Mountain, Yanshan Mountain, Duimianshan Mountain, Chulushan Mountain, Hulushan Mountain and Dashidoushan Mountain. These mountains line up like Triones and the village is named after the star. The stone houses in the village are differen from other places for beautiful colors and strong Southern Fujian style. Standing at the top of Doukui Village, you would find the view is even more beautiful than one could imagine.

石头厝人家 / the family living in the stone house

斗兴寺虽是新建，规模不小，工艺精妙 / the newly-built delicate temple

嵩口镇古民居的封火墙 / the fire seals of the ancient buildings

永泰县嵩口镇

　　嵩口镇位于福州市永泰县，当前古镇核心区由道南村、月阙村、中山村等村落组成，为"中国历史文化名镇"，镇上现有保存完好的明清古建筑100余座。

　　嵩口镇地处四市五县水陆交通要冲，早在南宋时期就已发展成为小集市，元代、明代时商业活动渐为繁荣，并逐步形成赶圩习俗。民国五年，这里成立了全省首家乡级商会，嵩口商贸重镇的地位得以确立，成了远近闻名的人流、物流集散地。嵩口古街、妈祖庙、大榕树，都成为嵩口镇的标志性景点。

　　随着水运的衰落，嵩口镇辉煌不再，但却保留了一批明清时期古建筑，主要有垅口厝、下坂厝、端公坂厝、下车碓、庵前宫、五显宫等明清时期建筑。古建筑里的石雕、砖雕、泥塑、彩画等等，民间工艺保存完好。

Songkou Town, Yongtai County

　　Songkou Town, be crowned as the famous historial and cultural town in China, consists of Daonan Village, Yueque Village and Zhongshan Village. There are more than 100 well-preserved ancient architectural buildings in the town. Because of its convenient transportation, Songkou Town had been developed into a small market in the Southern Song Dynasty. During the Yuan Dynasty and Ming Dynasty, the commerce developed rapidly and people from other towns would gather here to trade. In 1916, the first chamber of commerce with township level was founded, which demostrated its important status of commercial town. The ancient streets, Matsu Temple and the great banyan tree have become landmarks of Songkou Town. With the fading of water transportation, Songkou could not keep its glory in the past but it still preserve a number of ancient architectural buildings such as Longkoucuo, Xiabancuo, Duangongbancuo, Xiachedui, Anqiangong and Wuxiangong. Besides these wonderful ancient buildings, the stone carvings, brick carvings, clay carvings and pictures in the ancient buildings are all preserved in fine conditions.

嵩口镇古民居之龙口郑氏古厝 / Zheng's ancient house

保存完好的嵩口镇古民居 / the well-preserved ancient buildings

至今还有人居住，充满生活气息 / the well-preserved ancient buildings with dwellers

家用农具、明代古井 / the farm tools and the ancient well of the Ming Dynasty

精美门窗，点滴细节都是人间烟火味道 / the delicate windows showing the life

女儿墙，精美灰塑 / the low wall with grey sculptures

古镇上的老人 / the old in the ancient town

壁洲村全景 / Bizhou Village

关公信仰在壁洲村 / worshiping Guangong in Bizhou

连城县莒溪镇壁洲村

壁洲村位于龙岩市连城县莒溪镇，村中有"壁洲三宝"，广为人知。

首先，最著名的当为永隆桥，系明洪武二十年(1387)所建，距今已有600多年，是闽西尚存的古屋桥中最古老的一座。隔桥百步，是建于清康熙三十一年（1692）的文昌阁和天后宫，形成颇具特色的壁洲古建筑群。

文昌阁于清康熙三十一年(1692)动工兴建，至清雍正初竣工，由该村童生林上莘、吴勋一、黄林宴等10人(后人称"十友公")各捐100两银圆建成，以保该村风水。壁洲村天后宫坐落于文昌阁和永隆桥的中间，它始建于清乾隆末年，嘉庆初竣工。该宫为宫殿式砖木结构建筑，占地一亩多；天后宫的正门朝向莒溪，依次为门楼、天井、正殿。殿内供天后（妈祖）娘娘，这是一座典型的山区化的妈祖庙。

壁洲村历史悠久，还传承正月闹元宵、"二月二"游龙灯、船灯、"立春"时节游春牛等人们喜闻乐见的民间文艺节目，2012年，壁洲村被评为福建省历史文化名村、第一批中国传统村落。

Bizhou Village, Juxi Town, Liancheng County

Bizhou Village, located in Juxi Town, Liancheng County, is famous for Yonglong Bridge, Wenchang Pavilion and the Heavenly Goddess Palace. Yonglong Bridge, boasting a history of more than 600 years, was built in 1387. It is the oldest gallery bridge in Western Fujian Province. Within 100 miles, there are Wenchang Pavilion and the Heavenly Goddess Palace, which forms an architectural complex of Bizhou feature. Wenchang Pavilion, being built in 1692, was funded by 10 scholars in the village. The Heavenly Goddess Palace, between Wenchang Pavilion and Yonglong Bridge, started the construction during the last year of reign of Emperor Qianlong in the Qing Dynasty. It was finished years later. This palace, taking an area of more than 666.67 square meters, is a half timber palatial architecture. The palace, consisting of the gate house, the patio and the main hall, is of unique features in the mountain area. In Bizhou Village, a number of local festivals would be held during Spring Festival. In 2012, the village is crowned as Fujian Historical and Cultural Village and the First Chinese Traditional Village.

文昌阁外观5层，内实4层，一、二层方形，三层以上以悬臂梁构成八角形，顶为宝葫芦状 / Wenchang Pavilion

文昌阁里供奉"十友公"神主牌 / the Shrine of Shiyougong in Wenchang Pavilion

文昌阁里供奉的文昌帝君 / Wenchangdijun in Wenchang Pavilion

文昌阁平时开放底层，为当地村民休闲场所 / the ground floor of Wenchang Pavilion

文昌阁前雨坪建有荷塘，中建石拱桥 / the pond and the stone bridge in front of Wenchang Pavilion

文昌阁和天后宫形成壁洲村古建筑群 / the ancient architectural complex composed by Wenchang Pavilion and the Heavenly Goddess Palace

天后官内 / the look in the Heavenly Goddess Palace

天后宫内 / the look in the Heavenly Goddess Palace

石雕，细节之处见精美 / the stone carvings

永隆桥，始建于明洪武年间，为福建省级文物保护单位，桥名为原福建省委书记项南同志题写 / Yonglong Bridge of Hongwu Era in the Ming Dynasty being a provincial protection unit

桥内风景。永隆桥是壁洲村地标性建筑，也是百姓休闲、祭祀的重要场所 / inside the bridge

白石村地处梅花山腹地，是一座被时间遗忘的古村落 / Baishi Village—the ancient village in the depth of Meihuashan Mountain

连城县曲溪乡白石村

　　白石村位于龙岩市连城县曲溪乡，村子深处梅花山腹地的小山岗上，海拔1100米，三面梯田环抱，环境清幽，生态良好。白石村民居依山而建，错落有致，古香古色的吊脚楼，独居特色的田螺盖，村中小路多是青石板，鹅卵石铺就，曲径相连，纵横交错。白石村民以吴姓为主，早在明朝时，白石村先民就盖起了第一个祠堂——田螺盖，祠堂前有池塘，后有靠山，布局相当考究。白石村有溪沟三条，清澈溪流山间激荡，溪水灌溉周边的农田，同时也是白石村良好生态的保证，村里有红豆杉、长苞铁杉、柳杉、水杉等珍贵树种，形成一道天然屏障。远观白石村，如同一座被时间遗忘的古老山寨，古朴又不失别致、淡雅中又有一种安静的美丽，静静地沉睡在山涧中。

Baishi Village, Quxi Country, Liancheng County

　　Located in Quxi Country, Liancheng County, Baishi Village is in the depth of Meihuashan Mountain. With the elevation of 1100 meters, the village is surrounded by terraces and boasts a fine ecological environment. The residences in Baishi Village are constructed along the mountains, scattering in piecturesque order. Stilted buildings with antique flavour, the unique ancestral temple with the roof of the shape of the shell and paths paving with pebbles constitute the marvelous scene of the village. Most of the villagers in Baishi bear the family name of Wu. In the Ming Dynasty, the ancestors of Baishi Village built the first ancestral temple—the one with the roof of the shape of the shell. In front of the ancestral temple lies a small pond and at the back is a mountain. According to Chinese construction idea, the ancestral temple is well arranged. There are three streams running through the village, providing water supply for farmlands and plants. Inside the village, we could find various kind of rare trees, to name just a few, they are, yews, metasequoia. Baishi Village, being isolated from the hustle and bustle, is a delicate place with beauty.

护安桥里供奉"林陈李"三夫人，分别是林默娘、陈靖姑和李三娘 / three goddesses honored in Hu'an Bridge

护安桥内的宣传标语，记录一个时代 / the slogan in Hu'an Bridge

白石村护安桥，一座水泥铺面的廊桥，五进落，左边一落与公路相接，最右一落与山水相融 / Hu'an Bridge

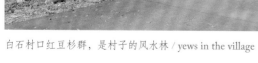
白石村口红豆杉群，是村子的风水林 / yews in the village

"文化大革命"时代的标语 / the slogan in 1970s

白石村第一代祠堂——田螺盖 / the first ancestral temple in Baishi Village

书坊建筑群 / the archite ctural complexes of the ancient printing houses

书坊水槽 / the water basin of the ancient printing house

连城县四堡镇

四堡镇位于龙岩市连城县北部，历史上，四堡镇地理位置并不理想，但曾是中国重要雕版印刷基地。当前，四堡镇重要的历史遗存主要集中在雾阁村和马屋村，四堡镇书坊建筑群、玉沙桥、雕版展览馆等等，都见证了中国古代雕版印刷的辉煌。1956年，郑振铎在厦门大学开讲座，就将四堡镇与北京、湖北武汉市汉口、江西金溪县浒湾并列为明清时期中国四大雕版印刷基地，而四堡镇则是其中保存最完整的一个，名列"福建省历史文化名乡"，2001年，幸存的古书坊建筑群也被列入了全国重点文物保护单位。

Sibao Town, Liancheng County

Located in the northern part of Liancheng County, Longyan City, Sibao Town once was an important block printing base in ancient China. At present, the cultural relics of Sibao are in Wuge Village and Mawu Village. The ancient printing houses, Yusha Bridge and Block Printing Museum are witnesses of the glory of block printing industry in Sibao. In 1956, Zheng Zhenduo, the famous scholar, quoted that Sibao Town, Beijing, Hankou and Jinxi County were the four important block printing bases during the Ming Dynasty and the Qing Dynasty. Sibao Town is well preserved and listed as Historical and Cultural County in Fujian Province. In 2001, the ancient printing houses were listed in Key Cultural Relic Sites under National Protection.

四堡镇因刻书致富，村中留存大量的青砖大宅，见证当年的辉煌 / the ancient residences in Sibao Town

四堡镇民居是典型的客家"九厅十八井"建筑 / the residence of Hakka style

厅堂是家族祭祀和举行重大仪式的活动场所 / the main hall of the residence

百年老宅只剩老年幼儿 / the kids and the old men in the village

四堡书坊建筑里随处可见的石槽，这是当年刻书黄金时代留下的痕迹 / the stone cistern

子仁屋门楼，始建于清嘉庆年间，为四堡镇有代表性的古民居兼古书坊 / the gateway of Zirenwu Building

四堡雕版印刷展览馆 / Sibao Block Printing Museum

花溪河上玉沙桥，始建于清康熙年间，为难得一见的精品廊桥 / Yusha Bridge

四堡镇忠显王庙，是四堡镇马屋村民为纪念先祖、东汉名将马援而修建的 / Zhongxianwang Temple to commemorate the famous general Ma Yuan

上厅龛台上是马援塑像，上悬挂"东汉一人"书匾；下厅建有戏台，戏台前是宽阔的天井，由鹅卵石铺成 / the shrine of Ma Yuan and the stage in the Zhongxianwang Temple

关帝庙 / Gugong Temple

马屋村以马姓为主，马氏家庙历史悠久 / Ma's Family Temple

四堡镇举行游神活动 / the parade of Sibao Town

正月期间，四堡镇都会举行游神活动，队伍穿街走巷，祈福平安 / the god parade held in Lunar January praying for peace

游神队伍从祠堂出发，穿街走巷，所到之处，鞭炮齐鸣，热闹非凡 / the parade team

中国四堡雕版印刷展览馆，为国家级重点文物保护单位。馆内收藏雕版以及古籍 / Sibao Block Printing Museum boasting of the engraved block and ancient books

展览馆内展示的雕版印刷流程和印刷工具 / the flow chart of block printing and printing tools

四堡镇锡器手艺人马恩明和他打制的锡器，该手艺在四堡镇传承已有百年，已被列入福建省省级非物质文化遗产名录 / the tin maker—Ma Enming and his tinwares

叩响时间 / knocking at the old door

上杭县太拔镇院田村

　　院田村位于龙岩市上杭县太拔镇，这里山水环绕，历史悠久，被列入中国首批传统村落。院田村客家古民居遍布，也是著名女诗人舒婷的第二故乡，对其创作影响深远，《致杭城》等知名诗篇就诞生在这里。

　　院田村的古民居雍容大气，有"九厅十八井，穿心走马楼"。村中至今留有"余庆楼""廓其有容""迎川至""生气磐郁""奠攸居""郎官第"等古建筑都称得上是大屋。近年来，当地在对村落进行抢救性维修保护的同时，着力挖掘其文化内涵，在舒婷旧居设立舒婷诗院，依托诗歌和客家文化，打造"诗意院田"文化品牌，在诗意中留下乡愁。

Yuantian Village, Taiba Town, Shanghang County

　　Yuantian Village, located in Taiba Town, Shanghang County, boasts a profound history and is crowned as Chinese First Traditional Village. Ancient residences with Hakka style scatter in this village. This village is also famous for being the second hometown of a well-known female poet—Shu Ting. When Shu Ting stayed in the village, she created some famous poems such as To Hangcheng. The ancient resideces in Yuantian Village mostly have nine halls and eighteen yards. There are some huge ancient residences in the village. In recent years, the local government focuses on the salvage restorations as well as the excavation of cultural connotations of those residences. For example, the government sets up Shu Ting Poetry to make the place well-known to the world.

院田村的建筑风格介于九厅十八井和客家五凤楼之间 / the construction style of Yuantian Village

石径小路，青砖黛瓦，院田村的古建筑群古朴典雅 / the ancient architectural complexes

褪色的门神、客家老人，还有厅堂上的照片，透出古村落的生活气息 / the washed-out pictures, Hakka old men and photos in the hall

空荡荡的宅子，诉说着时代的变迁 / the empty residence

奠攸居，始建于清代中期的古民居，保存相对完好 / Dianyouju House built in the Qing Dynasty

生气磐郁，舒婷旧居，朦胧诗诞生地 / Shu Ting's old residence

李氏家庙，院田村李姓居多 / Li's Family Temple

凌霄阁，始建于清代 / Lingxiaoge Residence

田背村至今保留有清代民居建筑近十栋，建筑风格多为"三堂、四堂出水"的大型建筑 / ancient residences in the Qing Dynasty

上杭县中都镇田背村

田背村位于龙岩市上杭县中都镇，已被列入中国传统村落名录。

田背村历史悠久，生态良好，村中建筑景观资源丰富，有始建于清代的宏文馆（文昌宫）、关帝庙，最有名当属始建于明嘉靖年间的云霄阁。云霄阁号称"中国斜塔"，外斜内正，共七层，下三层泥木结构，呈四方形，第三层起转八角形，全用木头架设，檩椽交错，结构精致，顶棚、窗棂、神龛上分别绘有龙凤图案，刻有花鸟浮雕，整座塔占地近400平方米，塔身高20米。近五百年来，云霄阁历经风雨而一直岿然不动。阁内藏有一大鼓，因老鼓长牛毛，吸引了专家学者前来探索，由此制作的专题片在中央电视台等媒体播出。

Tianbei Village, Zhongdu Town, Shanghang County

Tianbei Village, being listed as Chinese Traditional Village, boasts profound history, fine ecological enviroment and delicate architectual complexes such as Hongwenguan, Guangong Temple and Yunxiaoge. Among those architectural complexes, Yunxiaoge is the most famous because it is a leaning tower. There are 7 floors in this tower. The first three floors are square and made from clay and woods. From the fourth floor, it is transfered to octagon and made from wood. It is decorated with carvings of dragons , phoenixs, flowers and bird on the shrine. The tower, taking an area of 400 square meters, is of the height of 20 meters. Yunxiaoge has been here for nearly 500 years. Within this tower is an old drum which grows cow hairs. It attracts various specialists and even jounalists from CCTV.

经过时光的冲刷，已经难敌岁月侵蚀 / ancient residences being through the times

田背村中随处可见具有时代烙印的标语 / slogans in the village

始建于清嘉庆年间的宏文馆，又称文昌官 / Hongwenguan built in the Qing Dynasty

始建于清代的关帝庙 / Guangong Temple built in the Qing Dynasty

始建于明嘉靖年间的云霄阁，已经被列入福建省省级文物保护单位名录 / Yunxiaoge built in the Ming Dynasty

宏文馆中层层供奉的观音、魁星等神祇 / gods honored in Hongwenguan

宏文馆中精美的浮雕 / anaglyphs in Hongwenguan

鸢飞鱼跃 / flying birds and jumping fish

均庆寺是定光佛的祖庙，同时也供奉释迦牟尼和弥勒佛等神祇 / Junqingsi Temple

武平县岩前镇灵岩村

灵岩村位于龙岩市武平县岩前镇，已被列入中国传统村落名录。

灵岩村历史悠久，文物古迹众多。这里有一座形似狮子、浑然天成的山岩；同时，客家保护神定光佛、八仙之一何仙姑等，也与此地大有渊源。其中，福建省省级文物保护单位均庆寺为客家保护神"定光佛"的祖庙，定光佛信仰在海内外客家人中有深远影响，这里常年香火鼎盛。此外，一批古建筑群分布于狮岩南侧的村落中，这些建筑大多为清末民初的古建筑，既有客家特色的古建筑，也有浓郁南洋风情的骑楼建筑。

Lingyan Village, Yanqian Town, Wuping County

Lingyan Village, situated in Yanqian Town, Wuping County, is a Chinese Traditiaonl Village. Inside this village, one could find many historic sites and relics. A huge rock which looks like a lion is sitting in the village. According to the legend, Dingguangfo Buhhda and Goddess Hexiangu both share some conections with the village. Dingguangfo Buddha, who is the protector of Hakka people, influents Hakka people at home and abroad. Junqingsi Temple, where Dingguangfo Buhhda is honored, is the original one of all the other temples. Therefore, people would come here to honor their god. Besides these, a number of ancient architectural complexes built in the end of Qing Dynasty or at the beginning of the Republic of China are preserved well in this village. One could find out that these ancient houses are of both Hakka style as well as strong southeast Asia style.

均庆寺依托狮岩而建，为定光佛的道场，这也是闽西第一座被敕建的寺院，环境清幽，香火旺盛 / Junqingsi Temple – the place of Dingguangfo Buhhda

狮岩因形似狮，故而得名。岩有一洞，可容数十人，供奉定光古佛 / the lion rock

由于狮岩是喀斯特溶洞地貌，洞中有洞，现在供奉着客家人信仰的各种神祇，如关帝、何仙姑、药师菩萨等等，香火旺盛 / gods being honored in the lion rock

灵岩村所在的岩前镇，地处交通要道，建筑风格既有传统客家建筑，也有浓郁的南洋风情 / the mixed architectural style in Lingyan Village

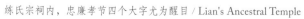
练氏宗祠内，忠廉孝节四个大字尤为醒目 / Lian's Ancestral Temple

练氏宗祠内，添丁人家都要往祠堂里送灯，以告慰祖先，家族人丁兴旺 / the families with newborns sending latterns to the ancestral temple

新罗区万安镇竹贯村

　　竹贯村位于龙岩市新罗区万安镇，2007年就被列入福建省历史文化名村，2013年被列入国家第二批传统村落名录。

　　竹贯村地处梅花山自然保护区南麓，是一个有700多年历史的古村落。在古代，村庄为联通各地的交通要道，随着时间的推移，道路变迁，竹贯村通衢地位不再，人迹罕至，渐渐被时间遗忘。也正是如此，竹贯村保留了一批颇有价值的古建筑群。元代温氏家庙、明代观音宫、清初关帝庙等10多处古迹保存完好，是目前福建省古迹群保存最完好的村庄之一。走进竹贯村，一条小溪贯穿全村，小桥、流水、人家、古寺、牌坊、廊桥……远山如黛，小溪清澈，仿佛置身在世外桃源。

Zhuguan Village, Wan'an Town, Xinluo District

　　Zhuguan Village, crownded as Fujian Provincial Hitoric Village and Chinese Second Traditional Village, is located in Wan'an Town, Xinluo District, Longyan City. Zhuguan Village, with a history of more than 700 years, is at the southern part of Meihuashan Mountain. In the past, it was a transport hub. As the time goes by, other roads were built and the glory of Zhuguan Village faded. It seems that the villaged had been forgotten by people. Thanks to it, the valuable ancient architectural complexes including Wen's Family Temple in the Yuan Dynasty, Kwan-yin Palace in the Ming Dynasty and Guangong Temple in the Qing Dynasty are all well-preserved. A stream wanders in the village. The bridge, jingling water, residences, ancient temples, memorial arches and gallery bridges make a fairyland in the world.

竹筛 / the bamboo sieve

老桥、小船、人家 / the bridge, the boat and the family along the stream

和大多数古村落一样，老人和儿童是村庄主力军，竹贯村也一样，村子人口以温、邓两姓为主，村民100多户 / the kids and the old men in the village

十二公王庵，又称积灵宫，始建于宋末，元至顺元年重修，一层供奉温姓先祖及幕像追随唐太宗在征战中有功的12位将军神位，因此又称之十二公王庵 / Twelve Generals Temple

观音庵，始建于明万历年间，一层供奉观音塑像 / Kwan-yin Temple

关公庵始建于清嘉庆年间，楼阁式庵堂，一层供奉关公塑像 / Guangong Temple built in the Qing Dynasty

温氏家庙，始建于元至正年间，明万历年间重修、扩建。坐西朝东，占地面积1200平方米 / Wen's Family Temple built in the Yuan Dynasty

温姓为竹贯村大姓，曾官至澎湖副将的温兆凤即出生于此 / people in Zhuguan Village bearing the family name of Wen

浪门金锁桥，又名保定桥，始建于清康熙年间，起名"浪门金锁"桥，意为锁住财富，其风格石砌单孔廊桥，南北向横跨村口竹贯溪之上 / Langmenjinsuo Bridge (Baoding Bridge)

保定桥历史悠久，是商贩走卒往返龙岩、闽北、闽中、闽南的交通要道。廊桥内设有靠栏，供行人休息，也设有神位，供路人膜拜祈福 / Langmenjinsuo Bridge (Baoding Bridge)

古香古色的精美雕刻随处可见 / the carvings with antique flavour

桥，成了村子最常见的风景 / the bridges being the most common scene in the village

曹氏宗祠又称永诜堂，这是一个四合小院落 / Cao's Ancestral Temple — Yongshen Hall

张氏族谱 / Zhang's family tree

漳平市赤水镇香寮村

　　香寮村位于漳平市赤水镇，2013年被列入全国第二批中国传统村落名录，拥有悠久的历史文化和众多的文物古迹。香寮村地处大山深处，生态极好，空气清新。香寮村也是有名的"百家姓古村"，自唐末曹、梁、傅、谢四姓开基至今，已有一千多年历史，现全村一千多人口中有近百个姓氏，包括少见的鹿、米、淑等姓。千百年来，香寮村民在这里怡然自得，在相互融合交往过程中创造了独一无二的"百家姓"优秀传统民俗文化。同时，香寮村也是伟大航海家王景弘的故里，境内还有耸峙云天的天台山以及天台庵、宋代石拱桥"凌云桥"等古迹。

Xiangliao Village, Chishui Town, Zhangping City

　　Xiangliao Village, listed as one of the Chinese Second Traditional Villages, boasts a profound history and abundant cultural relics. Since it is located in the depth of the moutain, the enviroment is quite good. The village was built by people with the family name of Cao, Liang, Fu and Xie at the end of the Tang Dynasy. It has a history of more than 1000 years. Some people in the village bear some rare family names such as Lu, Mi, Shu. For hundreds of years, people with different family names live in harmony with each other, creating an excellent folk customs. What's more, the village is the hometown of the famous navigators Wang Jinghong. Within the village there are a lot of historical sites such as Tiantai Mountain, Taintai Temple and Lingyun Bridge.

和大部分古村落一样，香寮村古建筑保存现状堪忧 / the ancient architectural complexes in bad condition

亟待保护的古建筑，尽管残破不堪，但仍保留着精美的砖雕 / the delicate brick carvings

古建筑大门，岁月侵蚀仍不失古朴。木雕也是相当精美 / the gate with antique flavour and the exquisite wood carvings

位于天台山森林公园内的天台寺 / Tiantai Temple in Tiantai Forest Park

宋代舍利塔 / the dagoba in the Song Dynasty

古桥、古驿道、古碑 / the ancient bridge, the ancient post road and the stele

双洋镇现存古民居建筑七十多座，多为清中后期所建，其中尤以东洋、西洋两村为多 / the ancient residences in Shuangyang Town

漳平市双洋镇

　　双洋镇位于龙岩漳平市，这里是福建省历史文化名镇。双洋名字的由来是因为当地有东洋、西洋二村，这两个村落历史悠久，保留了大量的历史文化古迹，其中东洋村更是被列入中国传统村落名录。双洋镇古时原为宁洋县旧址，明隆庆元年（1567）置县，于1956年撤销县治，存史389年。双洋镇有着深厚的文化底蕴，古镇既有风光旖旎的胜境，又留有大量的历史印记的古迹，有文庙、关帝庙、祝圣庙、廊桥、古民居等古建筑，周边的东洋和西洋等村落多处富有保存价值的古民居，保留原有历史风貌，民风淳朴。古镇留有"一塔二庙三戏四桥五堂"的人文景观，积淀着古朴风韵。明代大旅行家徐霞客曾两度游宁洋溪，在双洋镇嵌下了游历足迹和留下"程愈迫，则流愈急"的名句。

Shuangyang Town, Zhangping City

　　Shuangyang Town, crowned as Fujian Provincial Historic Town, derives its name from two villages–Dongyang Village and Xiyang Village in its region. There are a lot of historic sites in these two villages and Dongyang Village is on the list of Chinese Traditional Villages. In the past, Shuangyang was called Ningyang County which was established in 1567 and cancelled in 1956. Shuangyang Village boasts profound history, wonderful landscape and many historic sites such as Confucian Temple, Guangong Temple, Zhusheng Temple, the gallery bridge and ancient reisidences. Ancient residences are well-preseved in surrounding villages and it reveals the historic scenes in the past. The cultural sites of one tower, two temples, three operas, four bridges and five halls display the unique charm of Shuangyang. In the Ming Dynasty, Xu Xiake– the famous tourist visited Ningyang Stream for twice, leaving his footprints and famous poems right here.

现存的双洋镇古民居建筑类型主要为合院式民居，根据开间的大小，两房一厅的叫"三间起"，四房一厅的叫"五间起" / the ancient residences with a hall and several rooms

双洋镇古民居一般设有两重大门，厅坪外加横厝 / two gates outside the residences

怀德堂建于清代的古民居 / Huaide Hall built in the Qing Dynasty

时代的变迁，古建筑周围都盖满了现代建筑，还住在老房子的人已是少数 / few people living in the ancient residences

建于清道光年间的成德堂，号称有99间房 / Chengde Hall built in the Qing Dynasty

双洋镇的古民居建筑风格有明显的闽南风格 / the old houses with strong Southern Fujian style

老房子里的老物件，透出时光的气息 / the old things in the ancient houses

双洋镇的民居建筑注重装饰，精美的木雕、石雕、砖雕、灰塑、彩画装饰随处可见 / delicate decorations in the ancient residences

吴氏学堂（承启堂）建于清朝道光年间，历史上人才辈出，经过修葺，已对外开放 / the renovated Wu's School

双洋镇蕃衍堂，时代的标语与古代的牌匾并存 / Fanyan Hall

景德堂建于清代，现已修葺一新 / Jingde Hall

防溅墙上的彩绘至今鲜艳 / the paintings on the wall

文庙创建于明隆庆三年，明清两代均有重修，文庙大部分建筑都被改建为小学校舍，现仅余大成殿 / the Confusion Temple

双洋镇妈祖庙，屋顶上以嵌瓷为饰，色彩鲜艳，造型生动 / Heavely Goddess Temple

双洋镇有四座古廊桥。这是登瀛桥，建于清代，经过历代重修，现桥长33.8米 / Dengying Bridge – one of the four gallery bridges in Shuangyang Town

双洋镇麟山上耸立的"圆觉塔",也称"麟山塔",始建于明万历三十年（1602），是双洋镇最完整的古建筑遗物 / Lingshan Tower

麟山山顶的祝圣寺，香火旺盛 / Zhusheng Temple

丁屋岭海拔700多米，雨天时节，山寨云雾缭绕，宛如仙境 / the village in the mountains

长汀县古城镇丁黄村

　　丁黄村位于龙岩市长汀县古城镇，当地俗称丁屋岭，已被列入中国传统村落名录。丁屋岭处于海拔700多米的高山之上，未被现代文明侵扰，古村寨保持着原始的古朴和美丽。丁屋岭整个村落背风向阳，面山开阔。村中山寨民居独具特色。百姓建房都用本地特有的"丁屋岭页岩"作为材料，山寨吊脚楼随着地势，依山而建，高低起伏，错落有致。粗糙雄伟的石寨门，敞开式的老祠堂，清乾隆年间的老古井，无不向你讲述着丁屋岭的古朴厚重和自然生态。

Dinghuang Village, Gucheng Town, Changting County

　　Dinghuang Village, also named Dingwuling, is listed as Chinese Traditional Village. Dingwuling Village, isolated from the morden civilization, is hidden in the depth of the mountain. The village retains its simplicity and natural beauty. Facing the mountains, the village boasts fine geographical location. Houses in the village are of unique features since the villagers build their house with shales of the place. The stilted buildings are builit along the moutains, scattering in picturesque orders. The grand door, the ancestral hall and the old well are telling the history of this village.

"丁屋岭页岩"是村子建房铺路的主要建材 / Dingwuling Shales

丁屋岭依山而建，古民居高高低低，错落有致 / houses built along the mountains

正在修建中的寨门 / the door under construction

行走在丁屋岭，墙上的标语让人如同穿越时空 / the slogan on the wall

乡间祭祀 / the sacrfice of the village

城镇化冲击下的古村落，留在丁屋岭的居民不到百户，多为老人小孩 / kids and old men living in the village

丁屋岭敞开式祠堂，这里是村民活动中心 / the ancestral hall

崇文敬祖是客家人的传统，每到重大日子，都要祭神祭祖，请上戏班子，热闹一阵 / offering sacrifices to the ancestors

祭神祭祖 / honoring the gods and ancestors

一条小桥通向彭坊村 / a bridge leading to Pengfang Village

长汀县童坊镇彭坊村

　　彭坊村位于龙岩市长汀县童坊镇，村子因彭姓居多而得名彭坊。古时，彭坊地处长汀往四堡镇、清流县等地的古驿道上，至今村中有保留完好的明清古街，古街清一色两层小楼，楼下开店，楼上住人。此外，彭坊村有客家祖师叶伏虎成佛的神圣道场——千年古刹"广福院"；有千年古树——南紫薇；有丹霞地貌的"龙藏寨"；有原始森林"后龙山"；有明清遗风的"吊脚楼"；有客家风情的"古街坊"；有福建省省级非物质文化遗产"长汀客家刻纸龙灯"；有五百多年历史的"古石桥"等等。2013年彭坊村被列入龙岩市级古村落。

Pengfang Village, Tongfang Town, Changting County

　　Pengfang Village obtained its name because most people in the village bear the family name of Peng. In the past, Pengfang Village was in the post road from Changting to Sibao and Qingliu. In the village is a well-preserved ancient street. On both sides of the village there are two-floor buildings. The first floor usually is a store while the second floor is the house. In Pengfang Village, there is an ancient temple where Ye Fuhu attained Buddhahood—Guangfu Temple, an old tree about 1000 years old, the Danxia landform, the virgin forest, the stilted building, the old street, the provincial intangible cultural heritage—the papercut dragon lantern and the ancient stone bridge with a history of more than 500 years. In 2013, Pengfang Village is listed in Longyan Ancient Villages.

彭坊村是一个重要的驿站。世事变迁，古桥沧桑，来来往往的人不变 / the ancient bridge standing through the times

彭坊村至今还留存一条明清古街，传统的理发店、杂货店依然延续当年热闹 / the ancient street in Pengfang Village

宗祠是凝聚一个姓氏血脉的载体，每到过年，彭氏宗祠里总是热闹非常，当地人将彭祖奉为祖先 / people gathering in the ancestral temple during Spring Festival

彭坊村的祖师庙，这里供奉的是关公 / Zushi Temple in Pengfang Village

苏竹村全景 / the overall view of Suzhu Village

长汀县红山乡苏竹村

　　苏竹村位于龙岩市长汀县红山乡，被列入中国传统村落名录。苏竹村原名苦竹村，海拔近700米，地处偏僻，交通不便，因此保留了众多原生态的建筑。苏竹村建村于元代中期，是客家钟氏最重要的发源地之一。村庄至今还保留许多明清建筑，其建筑结构多以土木材料为主，苏竹村还保留许多石砌古道和古桥，整个村落古朴幽雅，自然与人文相融映衬，传承千年。新中国成立前，这里是前往长汀、连城、武平、上杭、宁化的重要通道，是一个易守难攻的战略要地。

Suzhu Village, Hongshan Country, Changting County

　　Suzhu Village, honored as Chinese Traditional Village, boasts a number of original buildings since it is hidden in a remote corner. Suzhu Village, established in the middle of the Yuan Dynasty, is one of the cradleland of Hakka Zhong's people. Until now, there are some residences built in the Ming and Qing Dynasty. These residences are mostyly made of woods and clay. Within the village are many ancient stone paths and stone bridges. Boasting the fine natural environment and profound history, this village is sure to be a nice place to visit. Before the establishment of People's Republic of China, the village is a strategic area that is easy to hold and hard to attrack sicnce it is an important passege leading to Changting, Liancheng, Wuping, Shanghang and Ninghua.

苏竹村内现存六口挖掘于明代的古井，分布在各处。井口均由大理条石围合而成，深度不一，至今仍是村民重要的水源地 / the ancient wells digged in the Ming Dynasty

苏竹村现存的建筑多为古老瓦房，其平面基本采用"三合天井"的合院建筑布局形式 / the residenes in the village

农家仓库 / the barn

苏竹村周围有一大片竹林，竹编农具在村子随处可见 / the bamboo forests surronding the village

历史上，苏竹村曾为交通要道。这是一座建于清代的供行人休憩的亭子 / a pavillion built in the Qing Dynasty offering a resting place for travellers

祠堂是苏竹村的重要建筑，先人逝世后，故居就成为后人祭祀的祠堂，上为应宗祠堂，下为井边祠堂，祠堂内的忠、孝、廉、节相传为宋代大儒朱熹所书 / the ancestral temple of the village

始建于元末明初的公王庙，清乾隆十年重修，庙宇以青砖砌成，保存较为完好，香火旺盛 / Gongwang Temple built at the end of Yuan Dynasty and the beginning of Ming Dynasy

小十四郎公祠，曾经为红三十六师师部旧址 / Xiaoshisilanggong Temple once being the site of the 36th military division of the Red Army

中复村一角 / a corner of Zhongfu Village

长汀县南山镇中复村

　　中复村位于龙岩市长汀县南山镇，已被评为中国历史文化名村。中复村位于长汀县与连城县的交界处，历史上，著名的"松毛岭阻击战"就发生在这里，当时村子作为红军后方，见证了众多红军子弟为苏维埃流尽最后一滴血。1934年9月30日，红九军团在该村的观寿公祠举行誓师大会，从这里开始了举世闻名的二万五千里长征。今天，在中复村可见当年的红军医院、红军桥、红军街和红军长征出发地等红色遗址。

Zhongfu Village, Nanshan Town, Changting County

　　Zhongfu Village, listed as Chinese Traditional Historic and Cultural Village, is located at the juncture of Changting and Liancheng. In the history, it was the home front of the famous Songmaoling Blocking Action. The village witnessed a great number of Red Army soldiers fought for sovietism. On September 30th, the 9th legion of Red Army held the oath-taking rally in Guanshougong Temple of the village and started the Long March afterwards. Therefore, we could find some revolutionary sites such as Red Army Hospital, Red Army Bridge, Red Army Street and the departure place of the Long March.

超坊围龙屋，始建于清代，典型的客家民居，松毛岭阻击战时，这里是红军战地医院 / Chaofangweilong House being used as Red Army Hospital

中复村老街，又被称为红军街，老街始于明代，繁荣于清代，为当年的交通要道 / the ancient street in Zhongfu Village

围龙屋占地面积有8000平方米，为典型的客家围龙屋，高峰时期曾居住70多户人家，如今多已搬离 / Weilongwu House with an area of 8000 square meters

尽管已经撤离，另建新宅，但村人把围龙屋里的老宅视为祖宅，逢年过节，还是要到祖宅贴春联，放鞭炮，祭祀祖先 / people gathering at the house to celebrate festivals

围龙屋中为数不多的几家住户，是城镇化大潮中仅有的坚守者 / people still living in the house

观寿公祠，这里是当年"松毛岭阻击战"的指挥部，也是红军长征的出发地，原为钟氏宗祠，已被列入福建省省级文物保护单位 / Guanshougong Temple

中复村古建筑中的抗日漫画，是难得的历史文物 / the Anti-Japanese Comics

接龙桥，也叫红军桥，当年扩红所在地，桥中供奉有真武大帝 / Jielong Bridge (Red Army Bridge)

岁月沧桑，残垣断壁，管窥当年风华 / crumbling walls and ruined curbs revealing the glory of the past

建瓯市徐墩镇伍石村

　　伍石村位于南平市建瓯市徐墩镇，这个村子以一处恢宏霸气的古民居群落闻名，这就是清末被誉为"建瓯西出第一家"的伍石山庄。

　　伍石山庄于清同治三年（1864）开工建造，至清光绪八年（1882）完工，历时18年，占地面积约9000平方米，由三大院落连成一体，民居建筑上吸收了徽派建筑和江浙民居的特点。民居外观整体性和美感很强，高墙封闭，马头翘角，墙线错落有致，黑瓦青砖，典雅大方。整个大院，布局严谨，建筑考究，规范而有变化，不但有整体美感，而且在局部建筑上各有特色，使整个建筑精美如诗，融古雅、精湛、富丽为一体。只是在岁月的侵蚀下，古民居群落已残破不堪，只剩断壁残垣，芳草萋萋。

Wushi Village, Xudun Town, Jianou City

　　Wushi Village, located in Xudun Town, is famous for a grand ancient architecutral complex–Wushi Villa. Wushi Villa, being establishedin 1864 and finished in 1882, takes an area of 9000 square meters. This architectural complex is consist of three big countyyards and absorbs the features of both Anhui and Jiangzhe construction styles. It is a great visual feast when you appreciate the house. With high walls and delicate eaves, this villa is sure to be a wonderful landscape. The villa is arranged in fine order and carefully designed. And each part of the buildings has its own characteristics, which makes the whole building looks even beautiful. It is a pity that this ancient architectural complex which is not preserved delicately is left in despair.

伍石村古民居仅剩的住户，依然延续传统的生活方式 / people in the ancient house still preserving their traditional life style

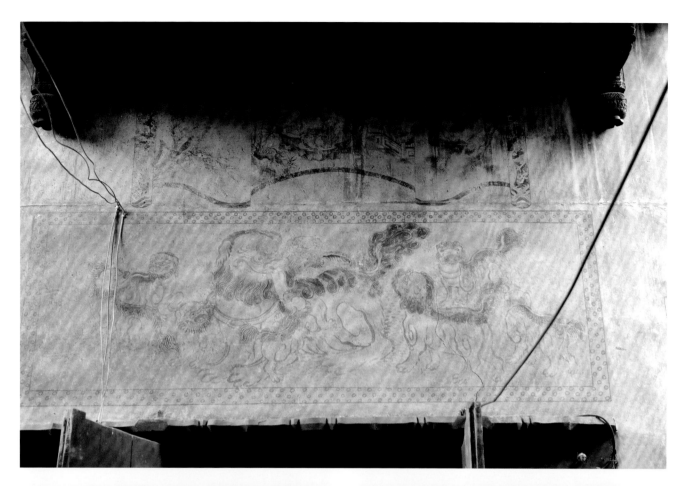

伍石山庄的壁画和古民居的雕梁画栋，依稀能想象当年豪宅的辉煌 / the delicate decorations of the house

精美柱础 / the delicate stone base of column

村中风水树 / the giant tree in the village been said to have magic power

建阳区莒口镇长埂村小源村

小源自然村位于南平市建阳区莒口镇长埂村，已被列入第四批中国传统村落名录。小源村历史悠久，开基于明代，距今已有五六百年的历史，为朱熹幼年老师刘子翚的后裔迁徙到此而建。村里的古建筑多为明清风格，历史悠久，文化底蕴深厚。"小源村"之名是刘氏后裔为纪念先祖与理学大师朱熹而取，"源"字便来自于朱熹《观书有感》一诗中的"问渠哪得清如许，为有源头活水来"。

小源村村庄不大，只有几十幢房子，依山而建，村口有一片风水林。村前一渠活水，汩汩流淌，村中，青石板的古巷中，有浅浅的小渠相随。村子古朴大方，书香浓郁。

Xiaoyuan Village, Changgeng Village, Jukou Town, Jianyang District

Xiaoyuan Village, listed in the Fourth Chinese Traditioanl Village, is esatblished in the Ming Dynasty by Liu Zihui's offsprings. Liu Zihui is the teacher of the famous scholar–Zhu Xi. Most of the ancient residences in the village boast a fairly long history and the costruction style are mostly of that in the Ming and Qing Dynasty. The name of the village drives from Zhu Xi's famous poem. The founders of the village wanted to commemorate their own ancestor–Liu Zihui and Zhu Xi. There are only a few houses in the village building along the mountain. In front of the village is a forest and a river. Within the village, little canals are hidden in the small alleys. It is such a great place for people to enjoy the leisure time.

小巷深深 / the meadering alley

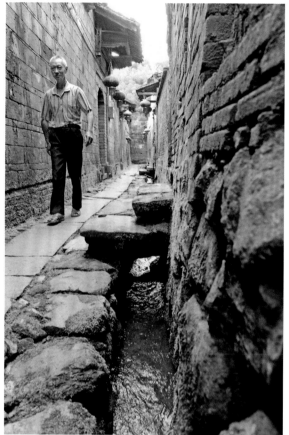

青石板铺路，小源村的乡村生活传统而宁静 / the stone path in the village

屏山书院，为刘子翚六世孙从五夫迁到小源村而建，现在是村中的祠堂 / Pingshan Study established by the 6th generation grandson of Liu Zihui

书院正中悬挂着刘子翚巨幅画像，厢房左侧，贴着族规、家训，院内立有四块清代石碑，记载着书院的历史 / the portrait of Liu Zihui in the middle

小源村的民居多为清代建筑，难掩岁月侵蚀 / residences built in the Qing Dynasty

厅堂、天井，陈旧但不失干净的古民居 / the hall and the yard

闲置用具，耕读人家 / the idle tools

精美窗棂，管窥当年繁华 / the delicate adjacent of window

九华庵，始建于清咸丰同治年间 / Jiuhua Temple built in the Qing Dynasty

在九华庵，每年八月十五都会举办庙会，热闹一方 / the annual temple fair held in Lunar August 15th

书坊村大宅楠木厅，门上石雕"妫汭传芳"表明主人姓氏是陈姓 / Nanmu Hall in Shufang Village

建阳区书坊乡书坊村

　　书坊村位于南平市建阳区书坊乡，在历史上，书坊和附近的麻沙镇是古代著名的雕版印刷基地，尤其是在宋代，这里有"图书之府"的美誉。当时，这里刻印的书被统称"麻沙本"或"建本"，与浙江临安刻印的"浙本"、四川成都刻印的"蜀本"齐名。

Shufang Village, Shufang Country, Jianyang District

　　Shufang Village, located in Shufang Country, is as famous as Masha Town in the history because of its book printing industry. In the Song Dynasty, it was even honored as "the Place of Books". At that time, books printed here are called as Mashaben Books or Jianben Books which is as famous as those produced in Sichuan and Zhejiang.

楠木厅建于清光绪末年，历时3年建成，精美砖雕是房子的一大看点 / Nanmu Hall built in the Qing Dynasty with delicate brick carvings

砖雕对联、双眼井，默默诉说当年繁华 / the couplet and two-hole well

古宅共用100多根楠木柱子，故而得名楠木厅 / Nanmu Hall constructed with more than 100 Nanmu poles

书坊村现存古建筑不多，但这里依然延续着缓慢的生活节奏 / the original life style in the village

在书坊村，时光仿佛静止，传统的理发老店，依然在等待客人 / the traditional barbershop waiting for the guests

蒲城县富岭乡山路村

　　山路村位于南平市蒲城县富岭乡，为闽江源头村。山路村地理位置偏僻，植被丰富，生态极佳。随着城市化的进程，如今村中仅剩不多的住户，房屋也大多人去楼空。留守的老人固守着传统的生活方式，节奏缓慢。

Shanlu Village, Fuling Country, Pucheng County

　　Shanglu Village, located at Fuling Country of Pucheng County in Nanping, is a village belonging to the headwater region of Minjiang River. Since it is far away from the hustle and bustle of the modern world, the environment of the village is under fine protection with abundant vegetation. With the process of urbanization, more and more villagers leave their hometown for a better and convenient life, leaving empty houses alone. Some old men who are stick to their traditional life style still live in the village, aging with the time at a slow speed.

生长 / the growing plant

溪水潺潺，生态极佳的山路村 / the village with a wondeful ecological environment

水泥路通到了村子，同时也让人走了出去 / the road leading to the village and evacuating the village

外出的人们只有春节回家，换上新春联又离开家乡 / the people working in the cities only coming back for Spring Festival

留守的老人 / the empty nester

福清山 / the temple on Fuqing Mountain

浦城县忠信镇坑尾村

坑尾村位于南平市浦城县忠信镇，村子在福清山中，风光秀美，古迹丰富。相传在隋朝以前，这里的福清山柘岭古道，就是中原地区联系福建的主要通道，唐末，仙霞岭古道开通之后，福清山柘岭古道才衰落。坑尾村也被称为"三江之源"的源头村，发源于此的涓涓细流分别注入福建闽江、浙江钱塘江、江西信江。

Kengwei Village, Zhongxin Town, Pucheng County

Kengwei Village, situated in Zhongxin Town, is hidden in the depth of Fuqing Mountain. Within this tiny village are a number of historic sites and wonderful landscape. According to the legend, it was Mount. Fuqing Zheling Ancient path which was used to connect the central plain area and Fujian before the end of the Tang Dynasty. After Xianxialing Ancient Path was brought into service, this ancient path is gradually forgotten. Kengwei Village is also called Yuantou Village since it is the headwater region of Minjiang River, Qiantangjiang River and Xinjiang River.

留守老人的生活 / the life of the empty nestors

村子里的每户人家，都有这么一个神龛，以敬天尊祖 / the shrine in the house

在坑尾村，时光停住了脚步，传统的生活在延续 / the traditional life in Kengwei Village

摩崖石刻鸿盘 / the cliff carvings

邵武市桂林乡横坑村

  横坑村位于南平市邵武市桂林乡，被列入中国传统村落名录。横坑村位于闽江源头，这里生态极佳，原名嵘衢坊，是由后唐工部侍郎黄峭后裔筑基建造，迄今已有1000多年的历史。由于横坑村地形酷似船型马槽，四周山势俗称"五马并槽"，东西南北中，各聚龙势，形态各异，跑、蹲、行、奔各自显威，曾兴盛一时。清朝时被人以一木横断其盛势，故横坑一名沿用至今。

  横坑村至今还较完整保留明、清时期各具特色的古民居建筑60多座,均为青砖碧瓦，纯一色明清建筑，大门和大厅门均以石条为框，门框三围浮雕松鹤、祥云。厅内百年壁画色彩依旧鲜艳，每扇门、窗上雕刻的图案各不相同，都非常的精巧。

Hengkeng Village, Guilin Country, Shaowu City

  Hengkeng Village, located in Guilin Country, is listed as Chinese Traditional Village. Since this village is at the headwater region of Minjiang River, it boasts excellent ecological environment. Hengkeng Village which was called Rongqufang is established by the offspring of Huang Qiao who was the assistant ministor of the Ministry of Construction in Later Tang Dynasty. It has a history of more than 1000 years. The terrain of Hengkeng Village looks like a ship-shape manger and the surrounding mountains looks like five horses. It formed a scene that looks like five horses eating in the same manger. According to traditional Chiense geomancy, it would bring prosperity to the village. And it did is quite prosperous at that time. Someone applied a tree in the middle and cut down its prosperity in the Qing Dynasty. And the name is shifted to Hengkeng. At present, there are more than 60 ancient residences in the village. Most of them are built with blue bricks and green tiles. The frames of doors are made from stone and decorated with raised patterns of cranes and clouds. Inside the halls are bright fescos and these fescos are different and delicate.

横坑村全景 / Hengkeng Village

始建于清代的"流芳"学堂，见证了横坑村科举时代的辉煌 / Liufang Study built in the Qing Dynasty been the evidence of Hengkeng schoolars briliant performances in the imperial examination

横坑村古民居大门多以石条为框 / most doors of the ancient residences being framed with long stones

横坑村古民居 / the ancient residence in Hengkeng Village

厅堂神位 / the shrine in the hall

横坑村古民居多为几进大宅 / most of the residences in Hengkeng having several yards

悬挂起来的生活 / the life hanging on the wall

柱础、石臼 / the stone base of columns and the stone mortar

石制水槽 / the stone sink

谷仓 / the barn

村子里的杂货铺 / the grocery shop in the village

水车，古村落的标志之一 / the water wheel – one of the symbols of the ancient village

黄氏宗祠 / Huang's Ancestral Temple

黄氏宗祠为邵武市南部最大的宗祠 / Huang's Ancestral Temple – the biggest ancestral temple in the south of Shaowu

黄氏宗祠 / Huang's Ancestral Temple

横坑村廊桥 / the gallery bridge in Hengkeng Village

老宅绿枝 / the green branch of the ancient house

笑脸常开 / the smiling face

笑看百年 / watching over the history with peaceful mind

邵武市沿山镇徐溪村

　　徐溪村位于南平邵武市沿山镇，已被列入全国乡村旅游扶贫重点村。徐溪村是沿山镇的一个大村，三条河流从村中穿过，村中至今保留有不少古建筑。徐溪村的古民居多为闽北传统建筑，基本都集中在街上，一色的雕花门楼，古朴典雅，令人遥想村子当年的繁华。只是在城镇化浪潮的冲击下，徐溪村也呈现出"空心化"趋势，村中剩下的也多为老人幼儿，令人一声叹息。

Xuxi Village, Yanshan Town, Shaowu City

　　Xuxi Village, located in Yanshan Town of Shaowu in Nanping, is listed as the key village of targeted poverty alleviation by developping tourism in the nation. Xuxi Village which is quite a large village in Yanshan Town boasts three rivers wandering throught and a great number of ancient architectures. The ancient architectures are mostly traditional buildings with Northern Fujian style and are gathered in the street. The elegant gateways with delicate decorations remind people of the past glory of the village. As the urbanization booms, Xuxi Village are also experiencing an awkard situation, that is, only the old and children are left behind in the village. It is such a pity.

高大的雕花门楼，岁月无声 / the magnificent gateway with delicate carvings

现代化冲击下，零散的古迹 / the scattered relics

母亲带着孩子走过古建筑的残垣，曾经风靡一时的广告词还留在墙上 / a mother taking her child walking past a wall with some popular advertisement

古制用具，显然已不用多时 / the tools of the past

厅堂风景 / the view of the main hall

厅堂风景 / the view of the main hall

普通人家的厨房 / the kitchen of a common family

元坑镇 / Yuankeng Town

顺昌县元坑镇

元坑镇位于南平市顺昌县，被评中国历史文化名镇。

历史上，元坑镇就是闽西北的交通要道，闽江三大支流的金溪贯穿境内，发达的水路运输让元坑镇成为明清时期有名的商贸中心。今天，元坑镇上保留有大量的明清时期的古建筑，多以祠堂、古民居为主。元坑镇的古民居大多为四进院落，高墙大院，雕刻装饰精美。走进元坑镇，整个古镇古建筑座座相邻，古井、古祠堂、古牌匾、古桥、古庙宇随处可见，具有很高的观赏价值和研究价值。此外，元坑镇上还有登云桥、文昌桥等古廊桥。

Yuankeng Town, Shunchang County

Yuankeng, located in Shunchang County, is listed as Chinese Historic and Cultural Town. In the past, Yuankeng, with Jinxi Stram passing through it, is an important route in Western Fujian. The advanced water trasportation in Yuankeng Village provided convenience to the birth of the important trade center–Yuankeng Town. Until now, there are a number of well-preserved ancient architectural complexes including houses and ancestral temples built in the Ming Dynsty or Qing Dynasty. Most of the ancient architectural complexes have four yards and delicate decorations. When you roam in the town, you could find a great number of old wells, old ancestral temple, old boards, old bridges and old temples. The small town is of great value in appreciation and research. Besides, there are some old gallery bridges such as Dengyun Bridge and Wenchang Bridge in the town.

雨中元坑镇 / Yuankeng Town in the rain

风雨亭 / Fengyu Pavillion

元坑镇古民居多为四进院落 / most of the ancient residences in Yuankeng Village having four yards

天井 / the yard

元坑镇陈氏古民居，又称陈氏三大栋 / Chen's Ancient Residence in Yuankeng Village

元坑镇天主教堂 / the Catholic Church in Yuankeng Village

吴氏宗祠和萧氏宗祠 / Wu's Ancestral Temple and Xiao's Ancestral Temple

池塘边的蔡氏宗祠和朱氏宗祠，都有装饰精美的砖雕门楼 / Cai's Ancestral Temple and Zhu's Ancestral Temple by the pond carvings on with delicate brick

每年的祭祖是元坑镇宗祠最热闹的时节 / the annual carnival for worshipping ancestors

新农村建设中兴建的文昌桥 / Wenchang Bridge

文昌桥为闽北最长的廊桥之一，桥中央供奉着神像 / Wenchang Bridge – the longest bridge in northern Fujian and the god honored in the bridge

精美木雕 / the wood carvings in the ancient residence

精美木雕 / the wood carvings in the ancient residence

角岭塔村就在崇阳溪边上 / Jiaolingta Village by Chongyang Stream

留守老人 / the empty nester

武夷山市岚谷乡客溪村角岭塔自然村

　　角岭塔是一个自然村，位于南平市武夷山市岚谷乡客溪村，是闽江源头村。

　　角岭塔村是个宁静而美丽的古村落，坐落在大山深处，崇阳溪的源头绕村而过。如今，村里的居民大多已经搬迁，村里仅剩下几户人家，继续着传统的生活方式。

Jiaolingta Village, Kexi Village, Langu Country, Wuyishan City

　　Jiaolingta Village, located in Kexi Village, is at the headwater region of Minjiang River. Since it is located in the depth of the moutains, the village keeps its tranquility and simplicity with Chongyang Stream embracing it. Most of the villagers have migrated to other places, leaving only few families who want to keep the traditional life style.

角岭塔村，最后的居民 / the last residence in Jiaolingta Village

红园村全景 / Hongyuan Village

武夷山市吴屯乡红园村

红园村位于南平市武夷山市吴屯乡，为中国传统村落。

红园村地处闽浙赣三省交界地，历史上曾是红色革命的重要根据地，新中国成立后，这里得名为"红园村"。红园村历史悠久，始建于明代，兴盛于清代，古时，这个村子是连接温林古驿道与岭阳古驿道必经之地。今天，红园村完整地保留了明清时期古村落的典型面貌，拱桥、石径、山涧、断壁残垣等村落风貌保存完好。明清时期盛产茶叶，是崇安当时的重要产茶区之一。由此，形成了妇女摆茶习俗，数百年以此睦邻里，敦宗亲，息争讼，弥纷争，构筑了独特的和谐文化景观，也是武夷山市珍贵的非物质文化遗产。

Hongyuan Village, Wutun Country, Wuyishan City

Hongyuan Village, hidden in the depth Wuyishan City, is a Chinese Traditional Village. It used to be the important base of Red Army. After the foundation of People's Republic of China, it changes its name to Hongyuan Village to commemorate the glorious history. Actually, the history of the village could be dated back to the Ming Dynasty. It was rapidly developed in the Qing Dynasty. In the past, it is the connecting place between Wenlin Ancient Post Road and Lingyang Ancient Post Road. The village boasts a well-preserved look during the Ming Dynasty and the Qing Dynasty. The arch bridge, the stone path, the streams and ancient walls in the village reaveal the profound history. Since it is a major tea production base in Chongan, an unique customs is formed, that is, Baicha. People use this customs to settle disputes between the neighbourhood and now it has becom a intangible cultural heritage in Mount. Wuyi.

几十年前的标语，时光在这里停住了脚步 / the slogans painted in decades ago displaing the history

红园村的日常生活 / the daily life of Hongyuan Village

古拱桥，岁月从这里流逝 / the ancient arch bridge

九龙村的土厝群蔚为壮观 / the magnificent clay houses

老屋 / the ancient house

延平区巨口乡九龙村

九龙村位于南平市延平区巨口乡，为福建省级传统村落。

九龙村地理位置偏僻，南面与古田县交界，村中有一座笔架山，为著名的旅游胜地。九龙村生态环境良好，空气清新，村中至今保留有大量的清代古建筑，其中最著名的当属这里的土厝群，这些土厝依山而建，连绵百座，远观相当壮观，有"小布达拉宫"之称。

Jiulong Village, Jukou Country, Yanping District

Jiulong Village, located in Jukou Country, is a Fujian Traditional Village. Boardering with Gutian County, the village boasts a famous tourist site—Mount. Bijiashan. When you walks in the village, you could enjoy the fresh air and fine natural environment. Inside the village are many ancient buildings built in the Qing Dynasty. Among those old buildings, the most famous houses should be those earth houses which are built along the moutains. Hundreds of eath houses are constructed in a cluster which looks like the Potala Palace.

老屋、老人、老木雕 / the ancient house, the old man and the old wood carvings

高宅深处，坦洋村曾富极一时 / Tanyang Village once being quite prosperous at a certain time

福安市社口镇坦洋村

　　坦洋村位于宁德市福安市社口镇，为中国传统村落，福建省历史文化名村。

　　坦洋村名最早见于清乾隆二十七年（1762）的《福宁府志》，因村形如长块木板，又称"板洋"。这里山清水秀，景色宜人，村中遍布茶园。坦洋村是驰名中外的闽红三大工夫茶之"坦洋工夫"红茶的发祥地，村内仍保留着古民居、古茶行、炮楼、廊桥、天后宫、施氏祠堂、胡氏祠堂等清代风格建筑。坦洋村民世代以茶为生，1915年"坦洋工夫"获得巴拿马太平洋万国博览会金奖。

Tanyang Village, Shekou Town, Fu'an City

　　Tanyang Village, situated in Shekou Town, is list as Chinese Traditional Village and Fujian Historic and Cultural Village. The name of the village first appeared in Funing Cholography in 1762. Because the shape of the village looks like a long board, it is also called Banyang. Boasting clear water and green hills, the village has a lot of tea plants. Tanyang Village is the birthplace of Tanyang Kongfu Tea. Inside the village are ancient houses, ancient tea shops, the gallery bridges, the block house, Shi's Ancestral Temple and Hu's Ancestral Temple. Villagers in Tanyang lives on the production of tea. In 1915, Tanyang Kongfu Tea won the golden prize in the 1915 Panama Pacific International Exposition.

碇步桥 / Dingbu Bridge

坦洋村因茶致富，村中不乏高院深宅 / a lot of big houses in Tanyang Village

坦洋村古民居 / the ancient houses in Tanyang Village

坦洋村天后宫和炮楼 / Heavenly Goddess Palace and the blockhouse

坦洋村口的真武桥，桥中供奉真武大帝 / Zhenwu Bridge in Tanyang Village

抽水烟的仙蒲村老人 / the old man smoking a water pipe

仙蒲村全景 / Xianpu Village

福鼎市磻溪镇仙蒲村 ————————————————————————

　　仙蒲村位于宁德市福鼎市磻溪镇，为中国历史文化名村。

　　仙蒲村在福鼎的西南部，这里是三县交界之地，田园风光秀丽，原始森林茂密，红豆杉、古枫林高耸，让整个村子显得宁静而古朴。村子建在深山里的开阔平地上，一条仙蒲溪穿村而过，村民临水而居，水中有鱼，人鱼和谐相处。仙蒲村现存有清代以来的古民居数十座，规模大，保存完好。古祠、古庙、古井构成古村落三大元素，其中林氏宗祠、林氏古民居等都是仙蒲村重要的历史遗迹。

Xianpu Village, Panxi Town, Fuding City ————————————————————————

　　Xianpu Village, located in the southeast of Fuding City, is a Chinese Historic Village. The village boasts an excellent environment with beautiful landscape. You could find a thick virgin forest, yews and old maples. The village is built in an open flat in the depth of the mountains. A stream winds through it. People constructed their houses along the stream and fish made their homes in the stream. What a harmonious scene! At present, there are ten ancient residences in the village. Most of these houses are rather big and preserved very well. The old ancestral temple, the old temple and the old well mark the history of the tiny village. Lin's Ancestral Temple and Lin's Ancient Residence are the historic place that one should take a look.

仙蒲村位于大山深处，村中古树林立 / Xianpu Village hidden in the depth of mountains

与闽东大部分村落一样，仙蒲村人鱼和谐相处 / the fish and people living in harmony

小桥、流水、人家 / the bridge, the water and the families

仙蒲村的古民居多为木板房，建在石头垒砌的台基上 / most of the residences being built on stone stylobates

仙蒲村的古民居 / the ancient residence in Xianpu Village

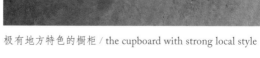

极有地方特色的橱柜 / the cupboard with strong local style

茶叶是仙蒲村重要的土产 / the tea being the specialty of Xianpu Village

仙蒲村的古民居大多有四角的庭院，宽敞整洁 / most of the residences boasting square yards

仙蒲村的古民居规模较大，气质大方 / the magnificent ancient residence in Xianpu Village

仙蒲村的大王公庙 / Dawanggong Temple in Xianpu Village

大王公庙里的神祇 / the gods in Dawanggong Temple

林氏宗祠，始建于宋代 / Lin's Ancestral Temple

仙蒲村古民居中的精美雕刻 / the delicate carvings of the ancient residences in Xianpu Village

金钗溪村地处古驿道的必经之路上，历史上是个富裕的村子 / Jinchaixi Village being quite prosperous in the past

福鼎市管阳镇金钗溪村

金钗溪村位于宁德市福鼎市管阳镇，为中国传统村落。

金钗溪村历史悠久，自古以来就是闽浙之交通要道。该村因村前有条金钗溪而得名，也有两种传说：一说是当年一位贵族乘轿经此，金钗失落溪中，故名；二是，因"金钗插地"而得名。村民大多姓朱，金钗溪朱氏始祖梦环公字符庆，南宋咸淳十年（1274）甲戌科进士，元兵灭宋，朱梦环不仕元，避隐金钗溪。

金钗溪村生态环境保护得不错，古驿道、金朱桥、土地庙、南天门、朱氏宗祠等古迹保存完好。村中的金朱桥连着古驿道，是往返柘荣和福鼎的必经之地，以前物流发达，是个富裕的村庄，当时这里客栈、商铺林立，有好几座质量较好的古民居。

Jinchaixi Village, Guanyang Town, Fuding City

Jinchaixi Village, boasting a profound history, is the on the route that links Fujian and Zhejiang. The village obtains its name from a stream—Jinchaixi Stream that wanders in the village. There are two other versions about the name. The first one is that some noble lady lost her gold hairpin when she passed across here. The second one is that a gold hairpin was stuck in the groud. Most of the villagers bear the family name of Zhu. The ancestor of these people is an official who served for the Southern Song Dynasty. After the Southern Song Dynasty was collapsed, a new dynasty was founded by invaders from the plain. Their ancestor didn't want to serve the new emperor, therefore he quited and hid in this place. Inside the village, there is fine natural environment and lots of historic sites. Since it is located between Zherong and Fuding, the village was quite prosperous in the past.

金钗溪古民居，多为两层木楼，称之为明楼 / the ancient residences mainly having two floors

位于村头的祠堂 / the ancestral hall

位于村头的祠堂 / the ancestral hall

古驿道和建于清代的土地庙 / the ancient post road and the wayside shrine built in the Qing Dynasty

朱氏宗祠，建于后山骆驼峰下，始建于明代 / Zhu's Ancestral Hall built in the Ming Dynasty at the foot of Luotuofeng Mountain

重新翻修后的朱氏宗祠，富丽堂皇 / the renovated Zhu's Ancestral Hall

朱氏宗祠屋顶上的彩塑 / the colorful sculptures on the roof of the ancestral hall

朱氏宗祠内保留的牌匾 / the tablets in the Zhu's Ancestral Hall

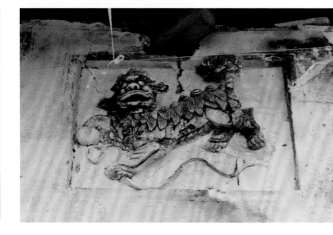

屋顶风景 / the view of roofs

精美木雕。雀替，八仙故事 / the decorated brackets telling the story of the Eight immortals

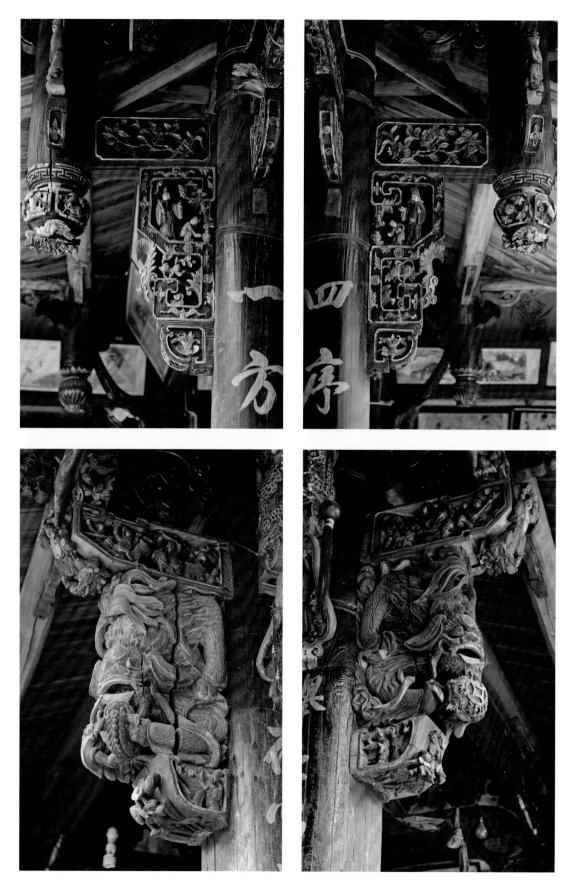

垂花柱、雀替 / the pillar with swags and the decorated brackets

金朱桥上的石碑，记载了多次重修的历史 / the stone tablet on the bridge recording the history

金朱桥，始建于清代，为福鼎古官道上重要的一个节点 / Jinzhu Bridge built in the Qing Dynasty being an important joint in the ancient post road

孔氏家庙 / Kong's Family

石碑 / the stone tablet

福鼎市管阳镇西昆村

　　西昆村位于宁德市福鼎市管阳镇，为中国传统村落，福建省级历史文化名村。

　　西昆村旧称狮崐村，历史悠久，曾是交通要道之一。西昆村作为江南孔裔第一村，有孔子后裔860多人，是孔子后裔在江南最大聚居地之一。作为江南孔裔第一村，保留有较为完善的孔子相关的文化与民俗，在福建名村中具有特殊性与唯一性，做到北有山东曲阜，南有福建西昆。村中目前保留清代古建筑30余处，其中规模大、工艺精、保存最好的有孔氏家庙、孔氏总厅（紫气东来）等九座。其中最具保护价值的是孔氏家庙，其保存完整，是全国为数不多的孔氏家庙，集中体现了闽东传统建造工艺的精华。

Xikun Village, Guanyang Town, Fuding City

　　Xikun Village is a Chinse Traditional Village and Fujian Provincial Historic Village. Xikun Village, used to be called Shikun, boasts a profound history and the convenient transportation. The most important is that villagers are the offsprings of Kongzi, therefore, it is addressed as the first Kong's Village in the south of Changjiang River. There are more than 860 Kongzi's offsprings in the village, which makes it the largest settlement of Kong's people in the south of Changjiang River. In the village, there are well-preserved related culture and fork customs which makes it differe from other villages. In the north, there is Shandong Qufu and in the south there is Fujian Xikun. There are more than 30 ancient residences built in the Qing Dynasty here. Kong's Family Temple, Kong's General Hall and other 7 buildings are the biggest, the most delicate and well preserved. Kong's Family Temple is of great value in protection since it is so well-prserved and reveal the essence of traditional architecture in eastern Fujian.

孔氏家庙，规模大，工艺精 / the magnificent and delicate Kong's Family Temple

西昆村为孔子后裔在南方最大的聚居地之一 / Xikun Village being the largest settlement of Confucius' offsprings in southern China

孔氏家庙中的牌匾，是西昆村科举时代辉煌的证明 / the tablets in Kong's Family Temple being the evidence of the glory at the imperial examinations

藻井 / the sunk panel

孔氏家庙二层戏台 / the two-floor stage of Kong's Family Temple

精美木雕 / the delicate wood carvings

精美木雕 / the delicate wood carvings

精美木雕 / the delicate wood carvings

精美木雕 / the delicate wood carvings

民间故事木雕 / the wood carvings of folk stories

精美垂花柱、雀替 / the pillar with swags and the decorated brackets

精美雀替、斗拱 / the delicate decorated brackets and the bucket arch

不同时代不同的印记 / the marks of different period of times

西昆村古民居 / the ancient residence in Xikun Village